Boston's Historic Places – So What?

An Interactive Guide for the Thoughtful Walker

Hilary Hopkins
Photographs by the Author

Jewelweed Books
Cambridge, Massachusetts

Boston's Historic Places -- So What?
An Interactive Guide for the Thoughtful Walker
© 2009 by Hilary Hopkins
All rights reserved

ISBN 978-0-692-00307-7

Library of Congress Control Number: 2009925673

Printed in the United States of America
Manufactured by BookMasters, Inc.
30 Amberwood Parkway, P. O. Box 388
Mansfield, Ohio 44805

Jewelweed Books
30 Winslow Street
Cambridge, Massachusetts 02138
617-491-8369
jewelweedbooks@verizon.net

Hopkins, Hilary 1938–
Boston's Historic Places -- So What?   An Interactive Guide
for the Thoughtful Walker/by Hilary Hopkins

For all those who came before
and all those who will come after

and, of course, for my elephant

TABLE OF CONTENTS

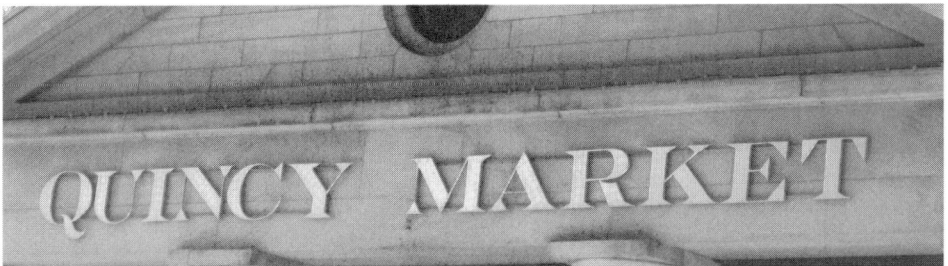

WELCOME

Hi, and welcome to Boston! As you walk her streets, looking, listening, and thinking, you will be walking the very same streets that Ben Franklin, Sam Adams, and John Hancock walked. Their presences are all around you along your way. If you turn your mind's eye back into the past, perhaps you will catch a glimpse of these heroes of our country. If you "listen" closely, you might also hear the voices of Boston's other citizens, the shopkeepers, laborers, seamstresses, and all the other uncelebrated folks, witnesses to the momentous events of their day, and as important to these events as you are to events current now.

HOW TO GET THE MOST FROM THIS GUIDE

There are many excellent guides and maps of Boston, and you should use them in conjunction with this book.

This guide, though, helps you participate actively in your travels along Boston's streets, to use your senses, your imagination, and above all your mind and your own experience and understanding to create an encounter with the historic sites of Boston that is yours and yours alone. You'll be invited to use blank spaces in this guide to write or draw--to make this book a record of your thoughts and dreams and ideas about the places you see, about your own home town, and about America.

And, of course, you're invited to have fun on your walk!

Begin anywhere you happen to find yourself in downtown Boston. Each of 25 historic places is presented on several pages of the guide. At the top of the first page for each place you'll find a theme to direct your contemplation of the site, followed by some information to help you understand its significance. Do use other fine historical guides to learn more if you like. This part for each site ends with a meditation for you to consider.

A page or two following the introduction of each site suggests ways to reflect more personally and actively on its meaning, by writing or drawing, or some other activity. There's plenty of blank space for your responses. By filling the blank pages with your own contributions, you make this book, and your travels on

Boston's historic streets, your own, different from anyone else's. If you are walking with family or friends, you can combine your ideas after some discussion and compromise. After all, discussion and compromise were and are important aspects of America's political and social life!

The historic places and buildings of Boston are much more than the sum of their bricks and boards, as interesting and significant as those are. They are spiritual centers, each one a focus for important, even noble, ideas and convictions. Stimulated by your walks in Boston, we invite you to explore your own important ideas, and perhaps to look in new ways at places in your home town.

Go upstairs at the Park Street T station to see this land. If the buildings were gone you could see all the way to the Charles River. It's never been built upon, and is the oldest public green in America.   A "common" is land owned by a whole community. (Note that Boston Common is always singular, never called "commons.")   In 1643 Governor Winthrop set aside 44 acres of land as a training field and pasture for cattle. For a long time, both uses continued--you can come any pleasant early morning and see people training in tai chi; and, until 1996, for a few days every June the New England Dairy Festival brought cows to pasture among the trees.

Through time this gathering place, like all such places across the world, has echoed to many different sounds. Listen, hear in your inner ear...

In the beginning, only the wind, the insects...birds...

1485. Eavesdrop on the soft conversation and laughter of Native American women and children as they draw water from the spring hereabouts.

1652. The sunny field echoes to the lowing of cows pastured here by Colonists. You can hear the crunching, chewing sounds the cows make as they graze peaceably on the grass.

June 1660. If you can bear it, hear the calls and sighs of the crowd gathered in the center of the Common to witness the hanging of Quaker Mary Dyer from the great central elm tree.

May 1766. A fine spring evening in more than one respect! The pealing of church bells and the whoomp! BANG! of fireworks delight the crowds assembled to cheer and celebrate the repeal of the hated Stamp Act.

1776. The Common echoes with heavy rhythmic footfalls and the chinking and clanging of swords and muskets as young British soldiers train and parade where the cows had been.

October 1783. The crackling sparks of a huge bonfire leap into the air amid the cheers and exclamations of thousands of people gathered to celebrate the surrender of the British at Yorktown.

June 1825. Join the cheers and exclamations of citizens and school children as the Marquis de Lafayette joins the great procession to Charlestown to lay the cornerstone of the Bunker Hill Monument.

1851. Cheer or jeer with the crowd listening to the strong clear voice of Amelia Bloomer speaking out in favor of liberating women's clothing.

1896. Hundreds of men with shovels dig a giant tunnel for the new Boston subway. They load the dirt on carts and horses pull the carts around the Common. They dump their cargoes of earth strategically in order to raise the elevation of the whole Common. Listen! the men call back forth to each other and the carts are creaking under their loads.

Around 1944. Clang! Thump! Rattle! The iron fencing that surrounds the Common is torn down and carted away to be used in the service of World War II.

October 1969. A hundred thousand demonstrators have marched and gathered here to protest the war in Vietnam on Moratorium Day. Their voices are raised in anger and frustration.

February 1978. The sounds of silence blanket the Common, as the Great Blizzard muffles all and the city slides to a stop.

October 1979. Above the sound of steady heavy rain, hear the voice of Pope John Paul II as he celebrates Mass here with 20,000 of the faithful.

December 31, last year. It's First Night, Boston's public New Year's Eve celebration! Lively crowds of all ages mill about the Common, enjoying art and music and food and blatting their big plastic horns to welcome the New Year.

MEDITATION
From their beginning, people have sought each other's company. Through the gift of the wonderful sounds we can make and hear, we have shared the events of our lives. Almost every place on the earth carries a weightless freight of layers and layers of human talk. Listen for the silent voices of places like this one.

FOR YOU TO DO AT THE BOSTON COMMON

Listen! shh now...and listen.

What do you hear, right now? Write down the sounds you hear to make your own sound picture of the Boston Common.

In your own home town, on what land do people gather for big events?

What sounds are heard there? What sounds have *you* heard, and made, at your home town gathering place?

Before you climb the stairs to look at this noble work of art that faces the State House, at the edge of the Common, stop and look at the back of the Memorial.

Near where you stand, nine hundred Black volunteer soldiers, led by twenty-five year old Robert Gould Shaw, son of a wealthy white Boston family, set out to sail south in the summer of 1863. At first the services of these men had been denied by the Army. Later, it was agreed they could fight--if led by white officers. Shaw, already a veteran, was the first to volunteer for this duty.

The 54th Regiment, the first composed of free Blacks, included two of the three sons of former slave Frederick Douglass, who had long lobbied President Lincoln to allow Blacks to serve; the Douglass boys were among the first to sign up for the 54th.

The men of the 54th were cheered on their way by an enormous crowd, doubtless including many of their proud yet anxious families. Alas! Less than two months later, at the siege of Fort Wagner in South Carolina, Shaw and most of his men were killed.

Here, on the back of the Robert Gould Shaw and 54th Regiment Memorial, are words which describe the determination and high purpose that are shown in sculpture in the memorial itself. Here are the names of those men of the 54th Regiment who gave their lives for principles they believed in: freedom, equality, union. Their bones lie mingled in a mass grave in South Carolina.

Take a few minutes to honor and remember those listed here by reading the account of their valor, and their names. As you read, the images that come to your mind will link you to these brave men, and them to you, if only for a moment.

Now climb the stairs and read about the Memorial, and see the faces that could have belonged to some of the names you read.

Are there fresh flowers in Colonel Shaw's lap? He and his men are occasionally honored in this way by some unknown person or persons.

MEDITATION

"...from these honored dead we take increased devotion to that cause for which they gave the last full measure of devotion--that we here highly resolve that these dead shall not have died in vain--that this nation, under God, shall have a new birth of freedom, and that government of the people, by the people, for the people, shall not perish from the earth."

--Abraham Lincoln, at Gettysburg, Pennsylvania, 1863

Shaw Memorial

FOR YOU TO DO AT THE SHAW MEMORIAL

What beliefs or devotions are so fundamental that they may over-come our natural desire for life?   We see a lot about deaths these days--violent deaths both real and dramatized. Sometimes these lives are given for beliefs or devotions, as was true on September 11, 2001, as difficult as it may be to accept that idea.

Do you know about any people who have believed or cherished something or someone so much that they have given their lives? Make a few notes to help you think about this.

Now turn inward, remembering the volunteers of the 54th Regiment, and the people you thought about above. Do you think there is anything you believe or cherish so much that you might be able to give your own life to preserve or support it?

Do these thoughts seem disturbing in some way? That is what such memorials are intended to do, to get you thinking. Are there similar monuments or sacred places in your home town? Maybe you could go visit them when you get home.

Here at the high edge of the Common is the imposing State House with its golden dome, built on land given by John Hancock (whose house was on the left front corner of the lot--you can see all that remains of it--its front steps).

These days, you cannot use the imposing main door, but if you go around to the right of it, you'll be able to enter. Once inside, take a moment to imagine that you are standing where perhaps John Hancock once stood!

You may think that arguments about the differing rights and responsibilities of state and federal governments are something new. But no. Here's a little story about this argument that goes back to the very beginning of our nation.

John Hancock was the first governor of Massachusetts, and he'd also been president of the Continental Congress that preceded the new United States Congress. When it was time to elect the first president of the new country, Governor Hancock thought it should be himself. When General Washington was chosen instead, Hancock was a bit put out.

Now, Governor Hancock was a fervent supporter of the rights of the new states, thought they should be quite autonomous. Although the new Constitution of 1787 provided for a central government, states were pretty suspicious of its powers.

When President Washington (aged 57) came to visit Boston in 1789, Hancock (aged 52) thought it would be appropriate for Washington to come first to visit him, being the governor of the state of Massachusetts. Washington, on the other hand, felt that the governor should come to *him* first, as the leader of the federal government. A standoff. Washington waited for a bit outside the city. Who was going to blink first?

Finally Washington agreed to continue his triumphal parade into the city. That evening as he ate dinner with his Vice-President, John Adams (aged 54), they waited in vain for a greeting from Governor Hancock. Not a word.

But political prudence prevailed. Later that evening Massachusetts Lieutenant Governor Sam Adams (aged 67) arrived to explain to President Washington that Governor Hancock had had a terrible attack of the gout, but would be able to visit him the next day. Which he did, wrapped in blankets, carried by several attendants.

Washington in turn politely agreed to come to tea at the governor's mansion. So bit by bit, in those beginning days, the relationship between state and federal power was defined.

Many politicians have come and gone in the State House since those earliest days. Most of them have been patriotic, public-spirited men and women with sincere though differing visions of the common good and an honest desire to try their hands at implementing it.

MEDITATION
"Government is nothing more than the combined force of society, or the united power of the multitude, for the peace, order, safety, good, and happiness of the people.."
    --John Adams, from notes for an oration to be given at
        Braintree, Massachusetts, in the spring of 1772, when he
        was 37 years old.

FOR YOU TO DO AT THE STATE HOUSE

Many offices and committees conduct the people's business in the State House and nearby state office buildings.   Here's a partial list of their concerns:

1-Black Caucus
2-Veterans' Affairs
3-Women's Caucus
4-Commerce and Labor
5-Election Laws
6-Housing and Urban Development
7-Human Services
8-Elder Affairs
9-Art Commission
10-Children's Legislative Caucus

11-Criminal Justice
12-Health Care
13-Science and Technology
14-Education and Humanities
15-Natural Resources and
    Agriculture
16-Public Safety
17-Transportation
18-Energy
19-Conservation and Recreation

Pretend you are a patriotic, dedicated, honorable politician, as you would be if elected, as the vast majority of elected folks are.

Without looking at the list above, choose a number from 1 to 19. Now look at the list to see what area of concern you've chosen. If you were in state government, what would law would you propose to improve services in the field you chose?

Now the hard part: how would you finance the establishment of your new law?

What objections to your proposed legislation might be raised? How would you address these concerns?

What do you think is the most important role of government?

Without a doubt, the issues you have addressed have been argued over many times within the walls of this building!

4   A SHORT DETOUR TO SOME INTERESTING BUILDINGS

Leaving the State House, take a short detour to admire some other buildings, along Beacon Street to your right as you face the State House. Staying on the same side of Beacon Street as the State House, just walk a block to the right and find a spot to pause across from the little red brick house. It's at the center of a lineup of six engagingly different buildings.

Usually when we walk alongside buildings we only look at their street level. But here's a great row of structures that rewards your upward gaze.

First, to your right at the corner, kitty-corner from the State House, is "Amory's Folly," the oldest of the six buildings, built in 1803 and designed by Charles Bulfinch, the great Boston-born architect of the State House and of the United States Capitol. At the time, this was the largest and grandest house in Boston. Alas, just before moving in, merchant Thomas Amory went bankrupt, and his imposing but abandoned home turned into a boardinghouse for politicians. See those two rows of black-bellied windows, and the protruding shops? In your mind's eye, strip them away to see the elegant simplicity of Bulfinch's original plan.

Next along comes the Claflin Building. Look up to admire its brownstone arches and the variety of carvings and trim at each level, and the windows cleverly angled for maximum light-catching. It's eighty years newer than Amory's Folly. In 1884 it was built for the then-new Boston University, to house their College of Liberal Arts. If you look closely you can see a "B" entwined with a "U" in the center of the ornamentation a couple of levels down from the roof. The Claflin family were major donors to the University, and that's them in the medallions above the main arch.

Right in front of you is another house, not nearly as grand as Amory's, but dating from almost the same time, 1808. Look across to its four slender columns and four stories, with windows that decrease in size at each level, in the Federal style of architecture. This used to be the home and studio (1827-1830) of a portrait painter named Chester Harding. Chester was known for his charm and his many clients. Nowadays Chester's studio is home to the country's oldest legal organization, the Boston Bar Association.

Squeezing Chester's on its other side is the Congregational House, almost a hundred years newer, finished in 1898. For sixty years it housed the library and the organizations associated with the Congregational Church, an early and important New England faith; the Library is still here. See those four bas-relief carvings above street level? If you have binoculars you can take a close look. Each has a theme and a 17th century date. There's "Rule Under Law by Consent of the Governed" (that's the Mayflower Compact being signed in 1620); "Worship According to Conscience" (showing the first Sabbath in America, also in 1620); "Education for Leadership" (the founding of Harvard College in 1636); and "Community Witness" (Preacher John Eliot among the Indians in 1642).

That dignified dark gray building next in line, Number 10-½ , is home to a great Boston institution, the Boston Athenaeum. This venerable library, open only to members, holds among its treasures the private library of George Washington. It may look a bit plain and even forbidding, but inside it's warm and welcoming. If you like, you can have a walk through parts of it. Just enter and get a visitor's pass. The present building dates from 1847 (the top two floors were added in 1915), so it was already here when the Claflin Building and Congregational House were built.

Now take just a glance past the Athenaeum, to see the last of the six, about nine stories high, of brick with some modest ornamentation. Although it seems rather anonymous compared to the others in the row, it too has a character, and speaks for the fashions of its time.

MEDITATION
Buildings speak a mute language. They invite or bar us, welcome, intimidate, or inspire us, just as people do. They represent values, too, just like people. A building can be like a story, or a newspaper, or a letter from the past.

FOR YOU TO DO IN FRONT OF THE ROW OF BUILDINGS

Remember how you used to make inanimate objects "speak" when you were playing as a child? What does each building seem to say for itself, or to you?

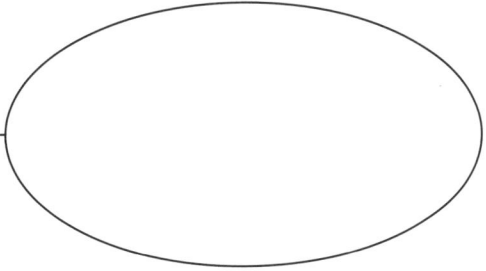

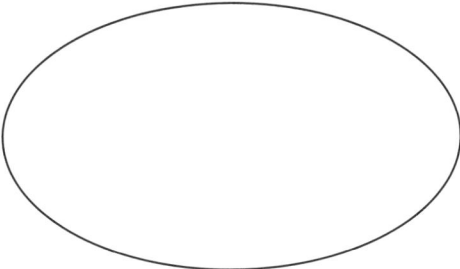

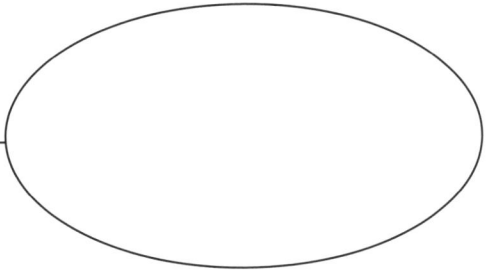

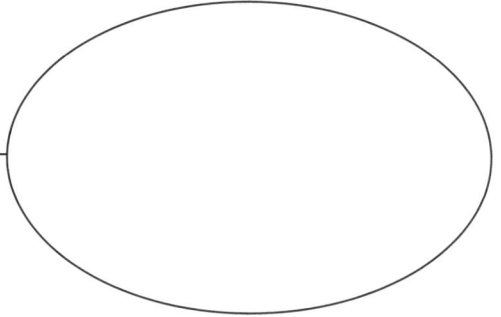

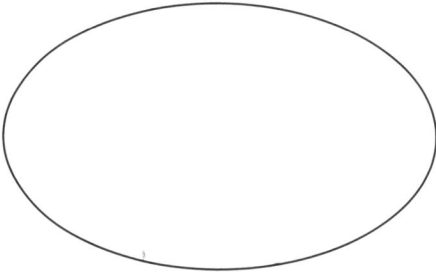

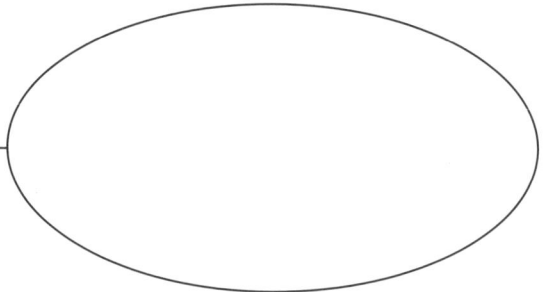

Why is it that the buildings seem to speak with different voices? What exactly are the physical elements of each structure which lead to their different "personalities"?

Interesting Buildings

5   PARK STREET CHURCH

A community that, like a catapult, has launched new ideas into the world

See the elegant tower of the church right in front of you as you exit Park Street T station.   Since its founding in 1809 it has fired new ideas into the community.   WHOOSH!! there goes one now--

1817.   WHOOSH!   Let's establish a religious school for our children. We'll call it a "Sunday School."

1819.   WHOOSH!   The natives of the Sandwich Islands [Hawai'i] need to hear the Word. Mr. Bingham and Mr. Thurston and others from our congregation will be leaving shortly to serve them as pioneer missionaries.

1824.   WHOOSH!   Our brothers in prison need assistance as well as punishment. Let us establish a society to aid them and their families. Who'll volunteer for this committee?

1829.   WHOOSH!   Slavery is wrong! Be at church July 4 to hear William Lloyd Garrison speak for the first time against this abomination.

Park Street Church

1831. WHOOSH! A new patriotic hymn has been written, called "America". Come and hear it sung for the first time on the front steps of the church on Independence Day.

1899. WHOOSH! Let's found an organization to care for our abandoned animal friends--after all, "Kindness Uplifts the World." We can call it the Animal Rescue League.

1923. WHOOSH! Say, everybody's listening to those radios now. How about we preach the Word on the radio waves!

1949. WHOOSH! Brother Billy Graham is coming to Boston for the first time. What better place for him to be heard than the Park Street Church?

2002. WHOOSH! Our inner-city youth need a special high school. Our church can take the lead to establish a school and help with scholarship money.

MEDITATION
Every new kind of undertaking requires courage. It is easier to invent new ideas if you have a community to help, from which to draw courage, and with whom to share unfamiliar tasks.

FOR YOU TO DO AT THE PARK STREET CHURCH

What's the hardest new thing you ever had to undertake?

How did you get up the courage to do this? What helped you? Who helped you? From what communities did you draw strength?

What advice would you give a friend who was trying do something new and scary?

1.

2.

3.

Have you ever said to a friend, "They should.../Somebody should.../Why don't they...?" Maybe you are the "they" or the "somebody."

What new thing needs doing in your community? How could you be part of it? Have you got the courage to undertake trying to fill a community need?

Adjacent to the Park Street Church, and next to the former site of a big town grain storage building, rest the mortal remains, and perhaps the spirits, of some men and women who were parents and midwives to the new nation, as well as those who were simply present at its birth.

Talents, money, convictions, passions, and intelligence were the birthday gifts of the parents and midwives. As for the rest, they lived the dailiness of their lives as best they could, trying to hold at bay their fears about the unsettled times. They played, worked, married, raised children, kept house, tended their domestic affairs--with much the same pleasures and worries as you and I have about all these parts of our lives.

Find the long low monument that marks the resting place of the Neal children. (Go straight into the cemetery, pass the large obelisk to your left, and watch to the right by the sidewalk for this stone; it faces the rear of the cemetery.) Consider for a few minutes the sorrow of the Neal parents. Twice they named new daughters Elizabeth, only to lose each baby at fewer than fifteen days of age, within five years of each other. They tried for a son, Andrew Junior. He also died, not even two years old. Imagine their heartbreak if you can.

Continue down this walk and turn left at the intersection. You will want to stop to pay your respects to the spirit of Paul Revere, Patriot, craftsman, and parent of the Revolution, whose marker is to the right.

In front of Paul's marker, turn to face the street and look in several rows for the awe-inspiring skull and crossbones on the monument of Elizabeth Hurd. Mrs. Hurd died at age 48. The stone tells how she was "very truly lamented by all her family and friends." Mrs. Hurd's husband was a Patriot, almost certainly a friend of Paul Revere's. The two families must have spent time together, would have shared the events of the Revolution. Mrs. Hurd must have worried for her husband during the war, and she died before seeing the Patriot victory. How sad for Mr. Hurd, not to have his "amiable and virtuous" wife to share his joy!

Continue down the walk and turn left at the intersection, so that you are once again facing the street. Just before you come to the tall obelisk honoring John Hancock, look for some small, low monuments to the right of the walk. Find that of Captain John Decoster, who died as a very young man of 26.

He says to you: "Stop here, my Friend, and cast an eye--
As you are now, so once was I!
As I am now, so you must be.
Prepare for Death, and follow me."

Who was left behind to mourn this young person? Parents? Brothers and sisters? perhaps a pet dog? buddies? sweethearts? fellow soldiers?

What did he look like? Blond? Brunet? Blue or brown eyes? How tall was he? What did he like to eat, to read, to do at play? What was the sound of his voice? There were those who knew it well...and missed its sound.

MEDITATION

Life's challenges, sorrows and joys change surprisingly little through historic time. Personal qualities that served our ancestors, whether famous or obscure, are as valued by us today as they were then.

FOR YOU TO DO AT THE GRANARY BURYING GROUND

Do you know Paul or John?

Paul was:
brave
flexible
patriotic
creative and productive
a good businessman
athletic, in great shape
good at inspiring workmen
enterprising
a risk-taker
confident
energetic
hard-working and practical
family-oriented
witty and quick
passionate
a maker of cannon, bells, cartoons,
  prints, dentures; items of gold,
  silver, and copper

John was:
self-confident
self-righteous
a shrewd businessman
a practical politician
adept at compromise
proud
intelligent, erudite
sociable and hospitable
able to take the heat
brave and defiant
visionary
conservative
well-liked
ambitious and calculating
socially adept
generous with wealth
an inspiring speaker

That's Paul Revere and John Hancock, both buried here.

Who do you know, or know of, who sounds like Paul?

Who sounds like John?

They were leaders of their day. What qualities do you think the leaders of, say, 2350, will need? any of these? different ones?

What does it mean, exactly, to be a "leader"?

With the Granary Burying Ground to your left, continue walking and shortly find the square-towered King's Chapel across the street. Building the original King's Chapel was a contentious business in 1686. Boston citizens did not want their valuable land sold to the British Anglican church, so the Royal Governor simply took the space by eminent domain (it was part of the burial ground next door). Resident British worshipped there; the Colonists shunned it for the most part. The old wooden structure was replaced in 1749 by the present granite church, finished in 1754.

Then came the Revolution. The Anglican rector fled, and the church closed for a short while. For a time a Congregational group shared the space with the now-Episcopal, formerly Anglican [British] original congregation.

They called it "Stone Chapel", though, so as not to have to refer to the King.

Here came James Freeman, a Harvard-educated man (who'd read some theology there but was not ordained). Freeman was asked by the Stone Chapel congregation to be their pastor. But there was a problem. Freeman profoundly disagreed with some of the basic tenets of the Episcopal faith. In fact, he was perhaps more Unitarian than Episcopalian. Let the congregation decide if I should stay, he thought, and preached a number of sermons on his beliefs. To his surprise, the congregation not only accepted him, but altered their worship services to conform to his beliefs.

That was not all. When the Episcopal Bishop refused to ordain Freeman as their rector, the upstart Stone Chapel congregation simply performed a lay ordination. And James Freeman continued as their minister for forty-three years.

During Freeman's long tenure, and in the generations to come, the Chapel's book of worship was revised many times. It is now completely unique to King's Chapel. However, many Anglican elements, both material and intangible, remain in the church and its worship.

The congregation of King's Chapel describes itself as "Unitarian in theology, Anglican in liturgy, and congregational in church government."

MEDITATION
Is it better radically to erase every vestige of the old as you embrace the new, or to be conservative and retain some elements of the old? What does it take to be a revolutionary?

FOR YOU TO DO AT KING'S CHAPEL

The congregation of Stone Chapel took matters into their own hands when the church authorities refused their request to ordain their chosen leader. They defied the established order and did as they thought best.

Yet several hundred years later many elements of that established order remain alive and important in the congregation.

Think about what you know about the American Revolution and what followed the break with England.

What of the old ways completely disappeared as a result of the Revolution?

What was retained from Colonial times or from the British presence in the Colonies?

Which things do you think were more important, those old ways that were discarded or the things that were kept?

What is the nature of the courage required to initiate, participate in, and live with a revolution?

Have you ever been a part of some kind of revolution--at work, at school, at home, in your town?

8 KING'S CHAPEL BURYING GROUND

Do we owe anything to the resting places of those who were important in the past? Or of anyone?

Boston's founding generation, and many subsequent generations, lie in this, our earliest cemetery (1630), next to King's Chapel. As you pick your way along the paths, see what graves you can find.

There's William Paddy, with the earliest monument (1658); he was born in 1600.

Charles Bulfinch, architect of the U. S. Capitol and the Massachusetts State House on Beacon Hill, has a marker in this cemetery, although he lies across the Charles River in Cambridge.

Mary Chilton, born in 1607 and thought to be the first passenger from the Mayflower to touch Plimouth Rock, lies here.

William Dawes, who together with Paul Revere and others made the famous "Midnight Ride," is here too.

Here's Rosanna Black, whose monument tells us that she was the "Virtuous and Amiable Consort of Mr. Moses Black." (A consort wasn't what you think; it's just another, gracious, word for wife.)

Find the monument adorned with a heart, memorializing Baby Martha Waye, only six weeks old when Death came for her.

There's Joseph Tapping's monument, with its amazing carved images of Death and Time.

British officer James Abercrombie, Jr. who led the final assault on Bunker Hill, is buried here, along with John Winthrop, born 1588, governor of the Massachusetts Bay Colony.

What's the most recent monument you can find?

MEDITATION
Do we owe anything to those long-gone to preserve their final resting places? Does it make a difference if they were "important" people? Why do we put markers over their graves?

FOR YOU TO DO AT THE KING'S CHAPEL BURYING GROUND

Why should we remember these people, anyway? or should we?

This graveyard has been through many changes in the past. What do you think of the way it looks today, as you explore it?

Here's some space to make a few comments.

Suppose you were in charge of the King's Chapel Burying Ground. How would you go about protecting the way it looks?

Some ideas for preserving and protecting the Burying Ground:
1.
2.
3.

How would you get the money to carry out your ideas? Where do you think the money should come from?

Some ideas for getting money to carry out your ideas:
1.
2.
3.

Suppose you were able to make some improvements, and the place looked even better! You want to re-dedicate the Burying Ground in some way, honor it. What kind of public ceremony would you plan? What would happen? Who would you invite?

Here's some space to imagine your rededication ceremony.

What about your own community? Are there historic sites at home that have come to be neglected, or are in need of protection? Is there anything you can do about that?

Resources are limited, though. Maybe you feel it is better to spend resources on needs of the present, rather than on things mostly important to history. What do you think?

How does a community decide what's important?

BOSTON LATIN SCHOOL SITE   What do schools
     BEN FRANKLIN STATUE   owe their students
     and communities?

Just around the corner from King's Chapel, on School Street, is the site of the very first school that was open to all, free (*if* you were a boy). Here you can play a favorite childhood game. In front of the ornate Old City Hall on the left side of the street, take a look at the sidewalk. See the hopscotch grid? The sculpture, by Lilli Ann Killen Rosenberg, hides wonderful tiny treasures to discover as you jump. It commemorates the establishment of the Boston Latin School in 1635.

At first the classes were held in the home of the schoolmaster, but in 1645 the first school building was built, right here.

Ben Franklin was a student, and John Hancock and Sam Adams, too. None of them would have been classmates, though--Ben was 16 years old when Sam was born in 1722, and Sam in turn was 15 years old when John was born, in 1737.

After your game, go into the handsome courtyard of Old City Hall and take a look at the statue of Ben Franklin to your left.

Ben is shown as an author, a statesman, a politician, and an inventor. Actually Ben dropped out of school, when he was only ten years old, to help his father. But during his brief time as a student, we can imagine that his basic character traits showed themselves and perhaps were nurtured or at least encouraged.

Ben was bold, curious, inventive yet pragmatic. He asked a lot of questions. He didn't hesitate to act on what he thought was right, what might work.

Well, maybe these traits *weren't* encouraged in school. A little boy of eight or nine who asks a lot of questions, tries to figure things out on his own, and goes right ahead and takes matters into his own hands when he thinks he's right--this student might have proved somewhat trying to the teachers of the time. They might even have been glad to see him go!

He turned out well, though, in spite of his lack of schooling. And he believed in education, even though he didn't have much of it.

Perhaps after all he did have a fine teacher, who recognized his gifts, supported and even celebrated them. There might have been someone who helped him form and channel his talents and inspired him to use them for the community's good and his own delight. That is the teacher we all would like to have had, for ourselves and for our children and our community's children.

MEDITATION
"An investment in knowledge always pays the best interest."
--Benjamin Franklin

FOR YOU TO DO AT THE BOSTON LATIN SCHOOL SITE AND THE STATUE OF BEN FRANKLIN

Oh, the teachers of our youth! We all remember at least one! Think back to when you were ten years old, the age Ben Franklin was when he left school, somewhere around the 4th or 5th grade.

Take a few lines to write the story of something that you remember about your teachers or school, in the 4th or 5th grade.

What values did this incident embody? *

Today, the Boston Latin School (yes, it's still in existence!) seeks to "ground its students in a contemporary classical education as preparation for successful college studies, responsible and engaged citizenship, and a rewarding life."

What values do you feel the schools in your community should encourage?

What about kids like Ben, who question, dare, and follow their own lead? How can schools encourage them? *Should* schools encourage them?

* Some values: tolerance fairness creativity humor charity decisiveness obedience rationality patriotism non-violence harmony spontaneity self-reliance prudence responsibility humility loyalty kindness restraint honesty consistency conformity

Continue walking past Old City Hall and take a seat on one of the benches at the end of the street, at the corner of School and Washington. Look over at the small handsome brick building on the opposite corner.

From 1982 to 1997 the Globe Corner Bookstore, this modest building went up in 1712 or thereabouts (following the great fire of 1711), and is only the second structure to stand on the site, one of the oldest buildings still standing in Boston.

Until the closing of the Globe Bookstore, there had been a bookstore here since the 1820's! At first it was owned by William Ticknor and James Fields, who for thirty years published the works of America's leading authors. Imagine the conversations that you could have overheard among the shelves: the two Henrys (Thoreau and Longfellow), Nathaniel Hawthorne and Ralph Waldo Emerson, Oliver Wendell Holmes and John Greenleaf Whittier, Harriet Beecher Stowe...

Annie Adams Fields, James' wife, played an important part in making this little building a literary landmark, too, by hosting the writers of the day at wonderfully intellectual social occasions and by including important women writers in these "networking" events.

In the 1950's, urban renewal offered a dire threat: let's raze this old brick wreck and build a parking garage!! But better ideas prevailed, and money came from many sources to allow the site to be purchased by Historic Boston Incorporated, a nonprofit organization dedicated to the preservation of endangered historic sites in the city.

Over the years this prominent commercial location has not only been a book business, but has also offered toys, pizza, boots, photo supplies, and gents' furnishings. It's housed a tailor, a hairdresser, and a coffee shop--not all at the same time, however.

What do you see there now?   What else is along the street?

MEDITATION
Cities are quintessential human inventions. From our earliest days we have relished coming together for commerce and conversation, goods and gossip. Enterprise, ingenuity, and business savvy made markets, villages, towns, and cities. The business of business keeps us lively and connected.

FOR YOU TO DO AT THE OLD CORNER BOOKSTORE SITE

Benches across from the Old Corner Bookstore site are a good place to rest the feet and the mind, and just take in the sights of the street and the passing scene.

Take a look up and down the street. List a few of the kinds of businesses and activities you see.

Now mark the ones you think might have been present in the 1850's, at the height of Ticknor and Fields' publishing career.

Below you can read a short list of some of the businesses here on School and Washington Streets in 1850, so you can compare then and now.*

accountant and copyist	apothecary
artificial flowers	auctioneer
fancy boxes store	bonnets and straw goods
bonnet presser	ladies' shoemaker
fur and cloth cap maker	daguerreotype maker
feather bed maker	fringes and tassels
gents' furnishings	hair dresser
ink store	livery stable
patent medicine store	portrait painter
umbrellas	West India goods
gilder	bookstores (26 of them!)

A note: Remember the importance of the horse in those days! You think the streets are littered now? Just imagine hundreds of horses doing their thing instead--and those long skirts ladies wore, dragging the ground...! No dry cleaners, either, and no washing machines. So much for the good old days.

* For comparison, here are some businesses from the same area in 1789: India goods, boardinghouse, bookseller and stationer, upholsterer, goldsmith, hatter, livery stable, leather dresser, watchmaker, grocer, apothecary, dentist, printer, saddler, paper stainer, tailor, blacksmith and farrier.

11 OLD SOUTH MEETING HOUSE

Standing at the site of the Old Corner Bookstore, look across the street to see the white steeple of the Old South Meeting House. "Meeting House" is a very appropriate name for the Old South. It's now a museum, but in 18th century Boston it was the largest meeting hall in the city.   Time and again angry citizens gathered here to air their grievances and argue the escalating issues of the day.   Imagine for instance the tumultuous scene on March 6, 1770, when Joseph Warren, standing before a furious crowd, denounced the shooting, only the evening before, of five Bostonians by British soldiers, just a short distance from the Meeting House--an event already dubbed The Boston Massacre. It would have been pretty hard to keep a cool head in such a crowd!

But possibly the most famous meeting in the Old South Meeting House took place on December 16, 1773.   Imagine the scene...

For many months in 1773 the Colonists and the British, represented in Boston by Governor Hutchinson and "tea consignees" (Loyalist merchants chosen to sell tea) have been attempting to reach an agreement about paying the hated tea tax, legislated by Parliament back on May 10.   Meetings are held. Committees are formed to meet with the consignees and get them to resign. None of them resigns.   Mob violence is visited upon at least one consignee. People are getting madder and madder.

In late November ships arrive in Boston Harbor filled with tea.   A "Body of the People" meet in Old South and insist that the tea go straight back to England, untaxed.   A day later another meeting rejects the offer of the consignees to just "store" the tea.

In mid-December, angry at learning that consignees in New York and Philadelphia have resigned, the Body of the People meet yet again to try to convince the owner of the tea ship *Dartmouth* to request permission from customs officials to sail away without unloading the tea.

No deal.   And if the tea isn't unloaded and taxed by midnight on December 16, the tea and the ship will be seized by Customs (and thus the tea remains in Boston).

On the morning of December 16, the Body of the People, five to seven thousand of them, gather in and outside the Old South.   A delegate is to be sent to the British Governor Hutchinson, requesting that he allow the tea ship to leave.

Governor Hutchinson is out in Milton that day, so it takes a while for his reply to be brought to the Body.

The Governor says No, the delegate reports late in the afternoon. And then the fateful words of signal, spoken by Samuel Adams:

"This meeting can do nothing more to save the country."   War whoops by the "Indians," and off they go to dump the detested tea into Boston Harbor.

Punishment by King George was swift and severe.   Boston Harbor, with its access to the outside world, was closed, followed a few months later by the rule of martial law in the city.   And followed, less than a year later, by the opening battle of the American Revolution at Lexington and Concord.   At least one of the "Indians" died in battle that day, the 19th of April, 1775.

That's the story.   But is it the entire story?   It's said that one third of the populace was for the Revolution, one third against it, and one third didn't care one way or the other.

How to decide where to stand?

MEDITATION
How do you weigh personal safety and security against your ideals? Where does your responsibility lie?   How do you decide what to do?

34   **Old South Meeting House**

FOR YOU TO DO AT THE OLD SOUTH MEETING HOUSE

Imagine yourself sitting in the Old South Meeting House on December 16, 1773, or standing in the crowd outside. Almost certainly most of the crowd were men, but women were there too.

Try placing yourself in each of the thirds. What would you think about the actions of the "Indians" as they tossed the tea into the harbor? What about throwing off British rule, i. e., actual revolution??

"I'm all for it!" (List a few reasons you might have.)
1.

2.

3.

4.

"I'm against it!" (Your reasons?)
1.

2.

3.

4.

"You know, I don't care one way or the other." (Why?)
1.

2.

3.

4.

Are there issues of the present day about which you can place yourself in one of these three groups? What would have to happen for you to move from one third to a different one?

If you walk past the Old South, keeping it to your right, shortly you'll come to State Street on your right. Look down it and find the Visitor Center for the Boston National Historical Park. It's on the right, across the street from the lovely little Old State House, number 13 in this book.

Here's a place to use the rest rooms, get a drink of water, ask the rangers on duty your questions, get a map or an interesting publication, sit for a few minutes.

This National Historical Park was established in 1974, in time for the Bicentennial, and includes eight sites directly associated with the American Revolution.

Three of these are owned by the Federal government: the Bunker Hill Monument, the Charlestown Navy Yard (where you will find the ship *Constitution*, Old Ironsides), and the Monument at Dorchester Heights (site of one of the last stands of the British in their siege of Boston).

The other five sites in the Park are owned either privately or by the City of Boston; the Federal government may assist them with funds for maintenance or restoration. They are: Fanueil Hall, the Paul Revere House, the Old North Church, the Old State House, and the Old South Meeting House.

Besides the eight sites of the Boston National Historical Park, you might enjoy visiting some of the other National Historic Sites in the Boston area. Here's some information about each of them, and public transit directions to them from the Boston Common.

ADAMS NATIONAL HISTORIC SITE. In Quincy, here you'll visit the birthplaces of Presidents John and John Quincy Adams and the mansion in which their family lived from 1788 all the way to 1927, as well as the church in which the presidents are buried.

Directions Take the Red Line to Mattapan and walk half a mile N on Burgin Parkway to Adams St.

BOSTON AFRICAN AMERICAN NATIONAL HISTORIC SITE. Walk the Black Heritage Trail to discover the fascinating history of the 19th century Black community on beautiful Beacon Hill.

Directions Pick up a brochure here at the Visitors' Center. Begin your walk back at the Shaw Memorial in front of the State House, and follow the black and brown signs.

FREDERICK LAW OLMSTED NATIONAL HISTORIC SITE. In Brookline, see the home and workplace of the father of American landscape architecture, designer of New York's Central Park and a multitude of other lovely places across the country. The peaceful wooded site offers a pleasant walk; in the house you may examine Olmsted's elegant plans, perhaps for a landscape near your home town.

Directions Take the Green Line (D) to Brookline Hills, walk 2 blocks S on Cypress St., then turn right 4 blocks on Walnut St. and left 1 block on Warren St. (after the church).

JOHN FITZGERALD KENNEDY NATIONAL HISTORIC SITE. In Brookline, return to 1917 as you visit the birthplace of the late president. It's as it was in the year of his birth.

Directions Take the Green Line (C) to Coolidge Corner. Walk 4 blocks N on Harvard St., then right 1 block on Beals St.

LONGFELLOW NATIONAL HISTORIC SITE. Cambridge, across the Charles River, was home to the poet and Harvard professor Henry Wadsworth Longfellow. Visit his gracious house with its pretty grounds, which was also General George Washington's headquarters during 1775–76.

Directions Take the Red Line to Harvard Square; walk 6 blocks up Brattle St.

National Historical Park Visitor Center 37

Other places to ask the Park Ranger about:

Lowell National Historical Park
textile mills, canals, lives of the "mill girls"

Minute Man National Historical Park
where the Revolution began

Salem Maritime National Historic Site
17th – 19th century waterfront

Saugus Iron Works National Historic Site
working reconstruction

Have fun!

Across from the National Park Visitor Center, what a fine surprise to come upon this elegant little building nestled here amidst the skyscrapers! The oldest public building in Boston, and one of the oldest in America, it dates from 1713. Although it now appears diminutive compared to its towering neighbors, as a symbol it is as big as the United States.

The Old State House has weathered many storms of history in its long life. It's echoed to the words of both the British Colonial government and the radical, "outrageous" voices of Massachusetts Patriots.

Built to house the Royal government, it also served as the meeting place for the freely-elected Massachusetts Assembly--a dual use which surely made for tense encounters in the corridors. Imagine the scene in the Council Chamber when in 1761 Patriot James Otis argued for eight impassioned hours against the Writs of Assistance (the "assistance" being for the British, allowing them to search homes without charges--we might call these "fishing expeditions" today). Of this speech, John Adams said, "Otis was a flame of fire...then and there the child Independence was born."

For the first time in the English-speaking world, citizens could gather to hear their elected officials, and judge their words--a right we take for granted today.

From its balcony the brand new, inflammatory Declaration of Independence from England was read to the assembled citizens, on July 18, 1776. In a delicious irony, in 1976, from that same balcony England's Queen Elizabeth II greeted the descendants of some of those same citizens, congratulating them on two hundred years of independence. Words, though they have no material substance, can have a power beyond measure.

For many years this precious building was given over to commercial uses. Yard goods and clothing were sold from its hallowed halls. Tailors and insurance agents set up shop. The offices of several railroad lines and an auctioneer and a stock broker and Western Union all found homes there. By 1870, over *fifty* different businesses gave the Old State House as their address!

In 1880, merchants suggested it be torn down--make more room for traffic, they said. Citizens in Chicago, hearing about this proposal, offered their own: they'd buy the Old State House and move it to the shores of Lake Michigan. Make a great tourist attraction out here in Illinois, wouldn't it?

That was too much for some local folks, who banded together the following year and lobbied and worked to save the building. Eventually successful, they called themselves The Bostonian Society and established the fine small museum now within the Old State House.

Although this lovely building is small, it has a weighty and significant history. Enter and listen for the words of our impassioned Patriots echoing through Time's corridors!

MEDITATION
Size is no indicator of importance.

FOR YOU TO DO AT THE OLD STATE HOUSE

Inside the Old State House is The Bostonian Society's wonderful museum, with exhibits about past and present Boston. There is a small entrance charge. It's a chance to come into a quiet, serene space, and have fun learning a few new things about history.

One way to really enjoy a museum, rather than just getting sore feet and glazed eyes, is to limit sharply what you look at. Try this:

In four or five of the dozen or so small rooms, choose just ONE object or display. Read, look, think only about it, and let the rest go for another visit. Move on to the next room, and do the same there. For each of your choices, pick one interesting thing you learned from it, and record that in the spaces below.

1. What I looked at:

   Something I learned from it:

2. What I looked at:

   Something I learned from it:

3. What I looked at:

   Something I learned from it:

4. What I looked at:

   Something I learned from it:

14 SITE OF THE BOSTON MASSACRE

The dangerous pleasure of righteous indignation

In the pavement of the small traffic island outside the Old State House you'll see a circle containing a star. Being careful of traffic, go stand on it as you read. You are standing on the site of the famous "Boston Massacre," a grievous affair as a result of which five Colonists died violently.

There are many accounts of the events of March 5, 1770. The drama was one of escalating tensions inflamed by exaggerated righteous indignation. It was a cold winter's night, the streets around you filled with dreary snow. A group of Bostonians was hanging around the British barracks, possibly on their way to or from the nearby Bunch of Grapes Tavern. The Colonials were daringly harassing the British soldiers, keeping them from entering their quarters; when one irritated, and possibly nervous, young soldier threatened the crowd with his bayonet, his captain hastily stopped him and got the soldiers into the barracks.

But that was enough for the crowd. Word of this incident spread quickly through the surrounding streets: "Did you hear? A lobstercoat used his bayonet on some fellows down by the Grapes!" "Gad! Did he kill 'em?" "Dunno-- I think maybe..." "Let's go see! Come on, Nate!"

About the time a bigger crowd began pour into these streets, a gang of boys was bravely hurling taunts and snowballs at a jittery British private, the lone sentry guarding the Custom House, a short distance away. He too finally threatened the kids with his bayonet, at which the boys, probably thrilled to get such a response, ran in several directions, some shouting that they were being attacked by Redcoats, and one to a nearby church, where he rang the alarm bells, usually reserved to warn of fire.

Shortly the poor sentry found himself facing a large, angry crowd all by himself. He held his ground, doubtless thinking he was going to be murdered where he stood. The Colonists, for their part, were enraged by what seemed threats to innocent civilians by soldiers who never should have been in their town in the first place. Their anger and frustration fed upon itself and enlarged.

Soon the British Captain Preston arrived with eight men; he tried his best to disperse the mob, assuring them his men would not hurt them. The furious Bostonians, taking safety in their numbers and their cause, cursed the soldiers and dared them to fire. One Colonist's account says, "...there was not the least provocation given to Captain Preston...the backs of the people being toward them when the people were attacked...Captain Preston is said to have ordered them to fire, and to have repeated that order."

Of course, we will never know precisely what happened, but one account suggests that when a British soldier was hit by a stick, he slipped on the ice and shot off his musket accidentally. In any case, the killing began: the Redcoats, pushed beyond discipline, fired twice into the crowd.

For every view, there is an opposite. Listen to the words of British Captain Preston: "I...heard...the most cruel and horrid threats against the troops...I was soon informed...their intention was to carry off the soldier from his post and probably murder him..."

Boston Massacre Site 43

"A general attack was made on the men by a great number of heavy clubs...by which all our lives were in imminent danger...on my asking the soldiers why they fired without orders, they said they heard the word fire and supposed it came from me. This might be the case as many of the mob called out fire, fire, but I assured the men that I gave no such order; that my words were, don't fire, stop your firing. In short, it was scarcely possible for the soldiers to know who said fire..."

MEDITATION

Each view that you yourself cherish is held equally dearly in its opposite by others. It does no good to work oneself up into a frenzy of indignation that such a thing should be true. We seek the comfort of others who hold our views, and from the safety of our group, wax righteous about ourselves, cutting ourselves off from our fellows who feel equally righteous. Better to try to find a meeting place, no matter how small, where we can all feel right together, try to reconcile our differences and work for the good of all of us.

FOR YOU TO DO AT THE BOSTON MASSACRE SITE

Pick a hot issue! On the privacy of this page, write your beliefs about abortion, gun control, welfare, women's rights, gay rights, immigration, affirmative action, or whatever current social issue really excites you.

Briefly, can you write why you hold these beliefs?

Now, for a challenge, present the view exactly opposing yours. Imagine that you really are a proponent of this view, and believe it as strongly as the one you described above.

Finally, for the most challenging exercise of all, search out a place, no matter how small it may be, in which you and your opposite might meet in agreement. What do you think you could *both* believe?

Congratulations! You have just taken steps to avoid the deadly dangers of righteous indignation!

The Government Center T stop will bring you here, or if you're at the site of the Boston Massacre, keep the Old State House at your left, cross the street, go up the small hill and walk right a short way to City Hall. It's not really a deeply historic building, since it was constructed in the 1960's, but it's worth a look.

Critics have likened City Hall Plaza to a red brick desert! It's true, it is rather daunting to cross in the dead of summer or winter, or in pouring rain. But when the Red Sox or the Celtics or the Patriots or the Bruins triumph (or whatever other delight needs celebrating), the Plaza is a fine gathering place for excited people.

But there's more here than meets the eye--as there is everywhere in a landscape. The bricks you are standing on have a special name. They are called Boston Pavers. For generations Boston has been a city of red brick, and these handsome multi-colored blocks are named in her honor.

Bricks are made of clay. A simple statement--but think of the countless questions it suggests. Who actually made an individual brick? Who made the machinery that helped the brickmaker in his or her work? We mean, What specific people? Their names? ages? appearance? families? where do they live? are they still living there? where's the brickyard? how much did they get paid for this work? On what day, exactly, was each brick made? where did it go after it was made? how did it get there?

Going one direction in time, before the bricks were made: what's the exact history of the clay that made a particular brick? "Clay" is what you call rock that's been eroded and eroded until its grains are no bigger than 0.002 millimeters across. Within what landscape did this clay lie? Imagine its history before it became clay: somewhere, a real place! deep in the earth, the rock was formed from which this clay evolved. Through how many eons of weathering did the rock have to pass before some of it was clay? If we could run an imaginary movie backwards, looking at our clay, what fantastic scenes would we see? Dinosaurs?

Going in the other direction of time, after the bricks were made, we can ask: Who were the bricklayers here on City Hall Plaza?

Their names? How long had each been working at this job? How did they learn their trade? On exactly what day, at what time, was a particular brick laid? What was the weather, that day? Since then, who all has walked across our particular brick?

Every object, natural or human-made, has a history!

MEDITATION
All the dailinesses of our lives--yours and mine as well as those of famous people--are embedded in the fabric of history. The plainest life, the most ordinary object, is a marvelous thread in the amazing tapestry of history.

City Hall Plaza

FOR YOU TO DO AT BOSTON CITY HALL PLAZA

Reach into your purse, pocket, or bag and take out the first object you touch.

What questions can you ask about its actual history, the history of its making, its origin, the origin of all its parts, the path by which it came to be something of yours? How far back in time can you reach with your questions?

My object:

Questions about it:

Now take a look around you, here on City Hall Plaza. Imagine for a moment that the buildings, cars, people, are all gone. Take a look back in time before Boston was here. What are the swells and dips of the land, under all those streets and structures? What trees or other plants might have been growing here? What animals? Are there any people? As recently as 1800, the water of the Atlantic Ocean came to within a few blocks of here, so your time-travel picture should include a shoreline.

Nobody's watching, so draw a little sketch of the City Hall Plaza landscape, say, 5,000 years ago. (Hint: there were native people here then.)

Say "Fan'l" or "Fan-yul" and you'll have it right. This elegant building with its statue of Patriot Sam Adams out front is now and has always been a spiritual and political heart of the city of Boston. Walk down the wide stairs at the right side of City Hall Plaza to visit it.

Peter Faneuil, formerly of New York, was by 1742 a rich, fun-loving merchant--he lived the single life since much of his money came in the form of an inheritance from his uncle, who made him promise he'd never marry if he accepted the money.

When it became clear that a central market building was needed in town, Merchant Faneuil offered to pay to have one built. Actually, not everyone wanted the big market. Street vendors feared it would put them out of business.

To sweeten the deal, Faneuil said he'd add a second story, for a public meeting hall. Construction proceeded and Faneuil Hall was accepted, and named, by city officials in August, 1742. Sadly, the first public meeting held in it was a memorial service for Peter Faneuil, who died a few months after completion of his market.

Following a huge fire in 1761, Faneuil Hall was rebuilt, and then enlarged in 1805, according to plans by the great architect Charles Bulfinch. Other rebuildings and refurbishings took place in 1899, in 1925, and in the 1970's.

Although for its entire history Faneuil Hall has had a market on its ground floor--first for meat and produce, and now--well, see for yourself--the upper floors have always been devoted to public affairs. The third story is the headquarters of the Ancient and Honorable Artillery Company, the third oldest military organization in the world., founded in London in 1537. If you are in Boston on the first Monday in June, you'll see the Ancient and Honorables in their annual muster on Boston Common.

But it's the second floor that seems to resonate with the voices of the people. Listen to words spoken here:

1765, James Otis, protesting the Stamp Act:
"We are told to be quiet when we see that the very money which is torn from us by lawless force [is] made use of...to feed and pamper a set of infamous wretches [meaning British soldiers] who swarm like the locusts of Egypt."

1772, Sam Adams:
"It does not require a majority to prevail, but rather an irate, tireless minority to set brush fires in people's minds. If ye love wealth greater than liberty, the tranquility of servitude greater than...freedom...crouch down and lick the hand that feeds you; may your chains set lightly on you..."

1824, General Lafayette, at a reception in his honor:
"May [Boston's] proud Faneuil Hall ever stand a monument to teach the world that resistance to oppression is a duty..."

1826, Daniel Webster, at the eulogy for John Adams and Thomas Jefferson:
"It is my living sentiment, and by the blessing of God it shall be my dying sentiment--independence now and independence forever."

1845, Charles Sumner:
"I cannot banish from my view the great shame and wrong of slavery...Its horrors who can tell?...Can this take place with our consent, nay, without our most determined opposition?"

1849, Frederick Douglass, speaking about his life as a slave:
"My mother and I were separated when I was but an infant--before I knew her as my mother...she died when I was about seven years old...I received the news of her death with much the same emotion I should have probably felt at the death of a stranger."

1960, John F. Kennedy, final speech of his presidential campaign:
"I believe in America where a separation of church and state is absolute...Where no church or church school is granted public funds or political preference...Where no religious body seeks to impose its will directly or indirectly upon the general populace or public acts of its officials."

2007, Judge Judith Dein, presiding at a citizenship ceremony:
"We are all much richer for knowing, living and working with people from other countries...It is a wonderful and difficult time to be a citizen...Hopefully, through debate and discussion, we'll have [immigration] laws that are fair to everyone...Our diversity is America's strength, not its weakness."

MEDITATION
"Congress shall make no law...abridging the freedom of speech; or the right of the people peaceably to assemble, and to petition the government for a redress of grievances."
    --Article I of the Bill of Rights (the first ten amendments to the Constitution, November 3, 1791)

Faneuil Hall   51

FOR YOU TO DO AT FANEUIL HALL

Here in this beautiful meeting space on the second floor of Faneuil Hall, quietly read aloud the stirring words on the previous pages. Imagine the crowds sitting where you are sitting, responding with their own thoughts and beliefs.

All right, now it's your turn. Suppose *you* had a chance to stand up at that podium, hallowed by our political ancestors, to speak for a few minutes on an issue of importance in *your* town or state.

What's your issue?

What three points do you want to make about your issue?

1.

2.

3.

(The audience is your local fellow citizens, magically transported to Boston.)

Here's a space to write your speech. Make it good!

You are a citizen of a city or town, of a state or district, of a nation, and of the world. Here in the United States, and in some other countries around our world, you have the legally-given right to speak your mind. It is more than a right, it is the most profound responsibility of citizens.

Claim your right and fulfil your responsibility to speak, to write, to discuss. Do not leave it to "Them." "They" are you. When you get home, make a promise to your community to be an active citizen, maybe once a month.

Imagine YOU, addressing this hall!

Faneuil Hall

The three elegant long buildings beyond Faneuil Hall are formally known as Faneuil Hall Marketplace, now that they've been recycled. They date from 1824, when they were the biggest development project of their day, devised by and named for then-mayor Josiah Quincy.

Always used as markets, with stalls for meat, cheese and produce sellers, by the 1970's the granite buildings were a rather disheveled part of a marginalized waterfront area. Enter architect Benjamin Thompson and developer James Rouse, whose plan for a recycled, rejuvenated marketplace finally won over the Boston Redevelopment Authority; by 1978 the vibrant cityscape you see here was up and running.

At the dedication of the "new" market in 1978, a skeptical visitor from out of state was heard to say, "It'll never work. No one will ever come here." Today, Quincy Market hosts more visitors every year than some famous amusement parks!

Take a break! Eat, walk, look at folks from all over. Buy a souvenir. Get a slice 1, get a sub 2, get some chowda 3, gelato 4, fried dough 5, galactoburrico 6, a gyro 7, salt water taffy 8, baked beans 9, a frappe 10, a stroller 11, some steamers 12, a lobsta 13 or some schrod 14, a calzone 15 or cannoli 16, a bottle of Samuel Adams 17 in his honor, or some tonic 18, and top it off with some ice cream with jimmies 19, or some Boston Cream Pie 20.

Huh?

Just some of our local food specialties!

1.   A slice of pizza.

2.   A huge sandwich on a long roll, often with cold cuts, cheese, and various condiments (called by other names in other parts of the U. S.).

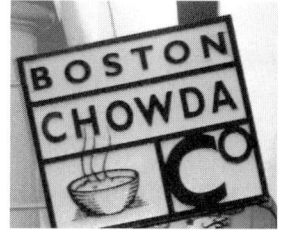

3. The Boston way of saying "chowder," in most cases clam chowder, made the Boston way with cream, rather than the Manhattan way with tomato.

4. A rich, dense Italian ice cream.

5. A large round piece of sweet dough, deep-fried into a delicate puffiness, often dusted with cinnamon and powdered sugar.

6. A Greek honey and custard pie.

7. Pronounced "yeer-ro", a Greek sandwich of meat, vegetables and yogurt sauce, wrapped in pita bread.

8. A kind of taffy containing salt, a seaside favorite.

9. Dried beans cooked slowly a very long time, seasoned with molasses.

10. Pronounced "frap." What the rest of the country calls a milkshake, with ice cream and flavorings. In Boston, a milkshake *has no ice cream!*

11. A kind of sandwich in which the filling is wrapped up in pita bread.

12. A soft-shell clam steamed in the shell, usually served by the bucketful.

13. The Boston way of saying "lobster".

14. Or scrod. Young cod or haddock. Some say that "schrod" is the haddock and "scrod" is the cod.

15. A calzone is sort of like a folded-over pizza.

16. A short tube of pastry, fried crisp, cooled, and filled with sweetened ricotta cheese.

17. Award-winning locally-brewed beer. It may be colored green on St. Patrick's Day, a holiday taken very seriously in Boston.

18. What many old-time Bostonians call any kind of soda/soda pop.

19. "Jimmies" are what Bostonians call chocolate sprinkles. Incidentally, Bostonians eat 50% more ice cream than folks anywhere else in the country.

20. A yellow cake in two thin layers, custard filling between them and chocolate frosting on top. NOT a pie!

MEDITATION
Maybe you are sitting where Mayor Quincy once stood to look at his pleasing big project. Raise a glass to our foresighted forefathers and foremothers!

FOR YOU TO DO AT QUINCY MARKET (while you are eating!)

Every region of the country has its own regional eating specialties. What's particular to *your* home town or state?

Breakfast foods? Sandwiches? Drinks? Pastries? Desserts and snacks? Ethnic foods?

18 NEW ENGLAND HOLOCAUST MEMORIAL

"If you look for the spark, you will find it in the ashes."

So said a Hasidic master, quoted by Elie Wiesel at the dedication of this memorial in 1995 (find it behind and left of City Hall). The spark lies within all, in each one of the six million dead and within each of us, sometimes hidden, but present nonetheless.

Here amidst the shadows and structures of American history stands a powerful reminder of evil and despair, and of sparks within ashes. The six towers, starkly illuminated at night, call to mind the six primary death camps, or the six million murdered.

The towers are etched with numbers from 0000001 to 6000000— so many, many numbers! Each number obscures a name, a name given in love to a baby boy or a baby girl, each baby an affirmation of life, arriving through pain into hopefulness, laughing and crying, learning and perceiving, being human. Murdered in pain, yet still alive even at the moment of death.

Read this story, told in the memorial, of a spark in the ashes:

"Ilse, a childhood friend of mine, once found a raspberry in the camp and carried it in her pocket all day to present to me that night on a leaf. Imagine a world in which your entire possession is one raspberry and you give it to your friend."
(Gerda Weissman Klein, deported from Germany as a teenager)

Each of the six million lives still, in the memories of those who knew them, and in the goodness of their acts, goodness which radiates from their ashes like the brilliance and warmth of a fire.

MEDITATION
Our memories of the people who have gone before us keep those people alive. By retelling their stories they live in us and, in turn, in those who know us.

FOR YOU TO DO AT THE HOLOCAUST MEMORIAL

Cast about in your memory banks for a person, long gone, whom you once knew--a friend, a relative, a neighbor. Write down the person's name.

Now bring that person to life again by remembering how he or she looked, sounded, acted. Your images may be faint, but as you focus on those gray ashes of memory, they may begin to glow a little more brightly.

Remember a little story about your person. In particular try to consider how something about this person lodged in your own self, and has affected you even if slightly.

Tell your person's story here.

What is it about your remembered person which has stayed in your own life?

Eighty or ninety years from now, what story would you want told about you? How will you have stayed alive in the memories of those who knew you, and, through their lives, how will your life have passed into lives of future people you will never know?

Cross the street now and face the Union Oyster House and the little alley to its left. At least, it's alley-like now, but in the 17th and 18th centuries it was a lively place.   Let's go back to those times...

If you'd been standing here in the 1640's, if you looked across to the left, you'd probably catch a glimpse of the large, shallow Mill Pond.   Much nearer to you, on your right, you'd see the Town Cove, deeper, where boats would dock and unload their goods. That would be exciting to watch!   The men are shouting and whistling to each other as they unload the big boxes and barrels. Some of them don't seem to be speaking English.   There's a nasty smell on the air, since local butcher shops dump their waste cuttings right in that little creek that flows where Blackstone Street is now.   You smell a kind of mucky smell, too, from the nearby marshes.

In 1714, if you wanted to see your eight-old friend Ben Franklin, you'd go to his home above his father's candle and soap-making shop, at the corner of Union and Hanover Streets, right nearby. Interesting smells in there!

Leaving the shop, you and Ben dodge the horse messes in the street and head back along Union Street, almost to Salt Lane and to the corner where the Capen family have their dry goods establishment (these days, it's the Union Oyster House).   New goods might be arriving here, and if you were lucky, Mr. Capen would let you carry a few things into the store.   The smell of the cloth is somehow foreign.   Some women are just coming in to the shop to buy some dress goods.   You hear a fragment of their conversation about the beautiful new State House that's just been built not far away.

Watch out for those carts rattling along the cobbled street, and those groups of our Continental Army soldiers!   It's 1779, and the soldiers are coming along to the house of Ebenezer Hancock there, at 10 Marshall Street.   Ebenezer is John's brother, and he has an important job as the deputy paymaster of our Army.

The men will probably walk down the little street to the Green Dragon Tavern to spend a bit of their pay. As you walk by the open tavern door you can smell the warm aroma of ale, and there's some smoke from pipes and a fire, and the odor of cooking, too.

MEDITATION
Open your imagination and your senses to return to the past!

Blackstone Block   61

FOR YOU TO DO AT THE BLACKSTONE BLOCK

All buildings and landscapes have a past. The house you live in, the building in which you may work, your neighborhood, your local park--all of these places with which you are familiar in the present must have looked different in the past--although in some ways things stay the same.

Take a look at the scene you see here. Choose a comfortable spot to stand, and make a little sketch of what you see--BUT leave out anything that you think would not have been here in 1714, when Ben Franklin was eight years old. Compare the present scene and your sketch.

What kinds of things change over time?

Why?

What kinds of things stay more or less the same?

Why?

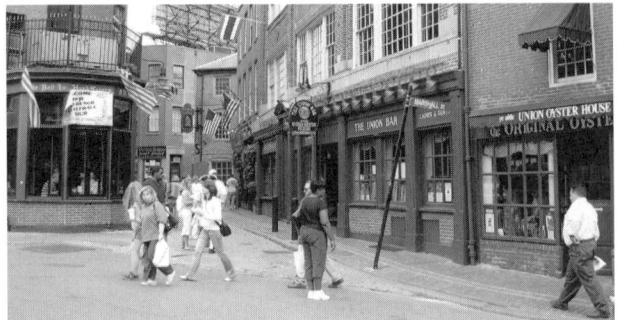

To find Paul's house from the Blackstone Block, walk down Marshall Street keeping the Union Oyster House at right. Keep walking, crossing the Greenway, to Richmond Street; take a right here, go one block to North Street, and take a left. Just up the street is the house.

Paul Revere lived in this house, all right--but it was already close to a hundred years old when he and his large family occupied it. In fact, this was the second house on this spot. A fire in 1676 destroyed the first house, home to the Puritan minister Increase Mather. Four years later, in 1680, a rich merchant, Robert Howard, built a new home here (this one), where he lived in some elegance.

Time passed; the smart new house became a bit old-fashioned. New owners renewed and updated it, adding a bit of height to accommodate a third story. But still, it was a nearly a century old when Paul Revere bought it in 1770.

Over the next twenty years or so the house was filled to bursting with Paul and his first wife Sara and their six surviving children, and his second wife Rachel and their five surviving children.   In the early 1790's the Reveres decided to move. They rented this house, moved to a larger one, and in 1800 they finally sold it.

Paul Revere died in 1818, the new republic he had helped to found grew stronger, and time marched on. The heroes of an earlier age, if not exactly forgotten, left center stage. This house served many purposes over the next hundred years: a tenement for new immigrants, with shops on the ground floor; a candy factory; a cigar factory; a grocery store. Each new use required some alterations to the building. Stories went up, stories went down. Walls up, walls down, doors cut, doors closed. Neighboring buildings down, up, down, up.

After this century of hard use, the little building seemed a prime candidate for urban renewal, and in 1902 the wreckers were about to take it down. In stepped Paul's great-grandson, John P. Reynolds, Jr. At the dawn of the American preservation movement, Reynolds and others recognized the value of saving and cherishing those monuments of our past which are instructive and inspiring. They formed the Paul Revere Memorial Association, and in 1907–08, after buying the house, initiated and completed its restoration, saving it from destruction.

Our sense of the dignity of history may be offended at the image of this building as a candy factory! But what would Paul have thought? He was a pragmatic person, a creative and forward-looking opportunist: if it's useful, use it.

MEDITATION
Which might be the way to go? A reverent preservation of significant landmarks of the past? Or a restructuring and reuse of what's outdated? Which better instructs the present and informs the future? How do we decide?

FOR YOU TO DO AT THE PAUL REVERE HOUSE

Way back in 1813, Philadelphia's Independence Hall, birthplace of the Declaration of Independence, was about to be torn down. In 1853, George Washington's home, Mount Vernon, was slated for destruction. In both cases, citizens came together to save these significant landmarks of our history. And here is Paul Revere's home, giving us a glimpse into our Boston past.

But maybe it's not that important to save these kinds of places. After all, they are just buildings. The lives of the people who inhabited them are more important than the bricks, aren't they? And besides, this is valuable land. Some homes could be built here for people living now, rather than two hundred years ago!

Try giving some arguments on both sides.

We should preserve old buildings because:
1.

2.

3.

We should renew/reuse/ tear down old buildings because:
1.

2.

3.

We should preserve an old building if:

We should renew/reuse/tear down an old building if:

In your town, have old buildings been preserved? If so, why? If you have visited one of these places, what did you learn from it?

Paul Revere House   65

From Paul's house to his Mall: keep the house to your left, go to the end of the block, go left on Prince Street, and next right on Hanover. Cross in front of a large brick church to enter the Mall.

This delightful neighborhood oasis, laid out in 1933, was paid for by funds given to the city by philanthropist George Robert White for the purpose of creating beautiful and useful open spaces.   At all seasons you will find a pleasant mix of local people and tourists enjoying the Mall.

You might be tempted to walk on through the Mall to the Old North Church, just beyond.   But there's more here than you might think at first glance. Stroll over to the left and take a look at the large panels on the brick wall.

The Mall is "Dedicated to the enjoyment of the community and to the memory of those men and women of the North End who helped to make Boston the pride of later generations," and on these plaques you will find a list of some of these North End citizens of years past.

Who were they? A volunteer in the Civil War. A tavern owner, a minister, an apprentice to a ship's carpenter. An artist, a college president and a school headmaster, a craftsman named Paul Revere. "The North End ship caulkers."   Although all those listed made their mark as adults, many of them had humble beginnings.

Rising behind the wall of plaques are some apartment buildings. Opposite, behind the wall to the right, is the Eliot School; it stands on the site of the North Writing School, founded in 1700, where boys, Paul Revere among them, went to learn elegant quill penmanship, the better to write important documents.

That was a long time ago. But right now, living in the apartments or attending the school, may be North Enders who will "help make Boston the pride of later generations."

Who's going to make your neighborhood proud?   You never know.

MEDITATION You may not know on what ground the seed is falling, so have faith as you sow it.

FOR YOU TO DO AT THE PAUL REVERE MALL

Do you know of someone who is/was an unlikely success?

Who?

What is/was the nature of his or her success?

What obstacles did this person have to overcome?

Situational obstacles?   Personal obstacles?

What qualities of this person allowed him/her to succeed?

Who in your neighborhood/school/workplace/circle of friends might be capable of great things?

And, of course, yourself: what encouragement have you received, perhaps from a surprising source, in making your own contributions? Who has had faith in you?

The Old North Church is at the far end of Paul Revere Mall.

"He said to his friend, 'If the British march by land or sea from the town tonight, hang a lantern aloft in the belfry arch of the North Church as a signal light--one, if by land, and two, if by sea--and I on the opposite shore will be ready to ride and spread the alarm through every Middlesex village and farm for the country folk to be up and to arm.' "

> (From Henry Wadsworth Longfellow's poem, <u>Paul Revere's Ride</u>)

The "he" is Paul, and his friend was the sexton, or custodian, of this church, named Robert Newman. Paul and Robert were friends. Paul was a Congregationalist, and this church was and is an Anglican/Episcopal church, so he was not a member of its congregation. But around 1745, when the church was about twenty years old, a peal of eight bells arrived from England for its belfry. Young Paul, along with some friends, signed a contract with the church to be its bell-ringers, and so he was quite familiar with the clergy and staff.

"The town" is Boston--the Boston Common to be exact, where during the tinder-box year of 1775 many British soldiers were encamped. The Colonials had lots of spies hanging around the troops, watching their movements and trying to pick up whatever information they could.

On the fateful day of April 18, 1775, word began to get out that the British seemed to be preparing to move, probably to go out west of Boston to some towns where the Colonials had moved stores of military materiel--gunpowder and so on--for safe-keeping. Patriot leaders Sam Adams and John Hancock had left the city and were out there, too, targets of the British. It would be important to know what route the troops were planning to take.

Paul and Dr. Joseph Warren of the Sons of Liberty, an activist Patriot group, knew that the North Church tower was the tallest thing around (it still is), and had laid a plan the weekend before, for just such an occasion.

You can imagine the conversation, perhaps at Sexton Robert Newman's home, away from listening ears: "Robert, Dr Warren and I need you to do something very important. It could be dangerous, with all these Redcoats around the streets. We think we are going to have a problem, and here's what we're going to try to do about it... So you see, once you get the word, if you can sneak up to the tower and hang the right number of lanterns, our "friends"--you know who they are--can see your signal and know the Regulars are moving, and which way. Would you be able to do that for us, do you think?"

Indeed, that night of April 18, Robert Newman hid near the church, and when he got the word, he quickly and quietly entered it using his sexton's key, locked the door behind him, went up to the tower in the dark, lit the two lanterns, and hastily left through a window at the far end of the church, so as not to be seen coming out by anyone on the street.

And at dawn the next morning, the first shots of the American Revolution were fired at Lexington Green, where Minutemen, warned by Paul Revere and his colleagues, were waiting for the British.

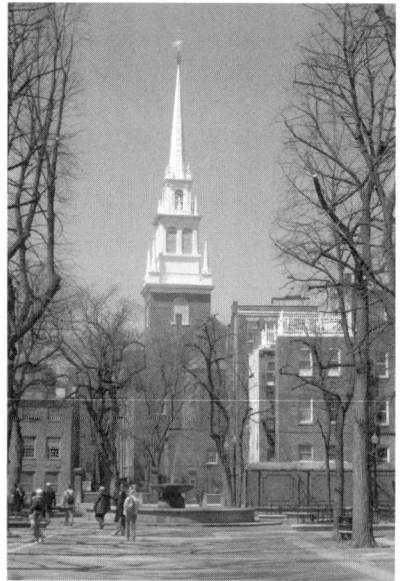

So this building is indeed an icon, a symbol of something sacred that is also itself regarded as sacred. Paul Revere walked where you walk now!

MEDITATION

An icon is associated with and represents something larger than itself. It embodies cherished beliefs and values and profoundly important institutions. Though it is symbolic, the icon itself also invites veneration. Think of the Statue of Liberty!

Old North Church

FOR YOU TO DO AT THE OLD NORTH CHURCH

Boston is full of iconic buildings and places, and you have seen many of them already.   They represent the hallowed stories of people and actions at the difficult birth of our nation. The spirits of our forefathers and foremothers inhabit these places, and we are fortunate that these iconic places are still here to hold those spirits.

But history is not only what happened a long long time ago. History will be what happened yesterday!

What more recent icon of American history can you think of? A person, an object, a building, a place? Something made sacred by its association with important, significant events?

Why is this iconic?

What values does it represent?

Is there a local icon in your home town?   What is it?

Why is it iconic? What does it symbolize?

Walk straight up the hill in front of the Old North to get to Copp's Hill Burying Ground.

Prehistoric Boston, and Old Boston, were places of hills, formed thousands of years ago by the action of the great glaciers. When they melted, some 16,000 years ago, they left behind the hills of Boston and its harbor.

Most of those hills were actually leveled during Boston's earliest years, to fill in marshes (such as those around the Blackstone Block). Some, however, were let to stand: Beacon Hill (though much reduced), Breed's Hill and Bunker Hill across the harbor in Charlestown, and the hill you are now standing on, Copp's Hill.

From 1660, this cemetery has served the residents of the North End of Boston. Before it became a cemetery, though, it had a windmill on it--doubtless an excellent location since it was the highest land around. William Copp farmed on its banks, too, and his grandsons are buried in the cemetery. Many of Boston's earliest Black citizens were buried here; the nearby Black community was called New Guinea. The grave of Robert Newman- -Paul Revere's friend the sexton of Old North Church--is here also, as are the graves of many members of the illustrious Mather family of religious note.

As a cemetery it filled up quickly, and adjacent land was added to enlarge it.   By the time of the Revolution it was close to its present size, a fine vantage point from which to look across the harbor to the hills of Charlestown.

And that is where the British artillery were looking, on the morning of June 17, 1775--just two months after the first shots were fired in Lexington. A fierce battle was being waged across the water, the rebels dug in at the top of Breed's Hill (erroneously and ever after called Bunker Hill), the British troops laying siege to them. From here on Copp's Hill, with its excellent view, the British cannon fired again and again, eventually setting fire to Charlestown and burning it down.

British General Burgoyne described the scene with satisfaction: "...one of the greatest scenes of war that can be conceived...before us a great and noble town in one great blaze--the church steeples, being timber, were great triangles of fire above the rest; behind us the church steeples and heights of our own camp covered with spectators...the roar of cannon, mortars and musquetry..."

They all came up here to look.

MEDITATION

From a vantage point you can see all around you. But what you see depends on where you look, where you stand, and what you are looking for. Can a vantage point be not a place but an attitude?

FOR YOU TO DO AT COPP'S HILL BURYING GROUND

It's 1475, and you're a Native American, standing on top of this hill and looking around in all directions. What are you looking for? What do you see? What do you NOT see?

It's 1675. You're coming up the hill for the burial of your beloved relative in the cemetery here. What do you hope you will see? What do you notice from up here?

It's June 17, 1775. You are a British officer planning how best to attack Charlestown. What do you think about being up on this hill? What are your plans?

It's June 1975, and you are a North Ender who lives across the street. What do you see on Copp's Hill? When you go over there, what do you look at?

Now, consider a vantage point in your home town, a place which gives a view--a hill or a building. What is its history? What do you see when you are standing on it?

What kind of *mental* vantage point allows you to see most clearly?

Leaving Copp's Hill, go left straight down; at the bottom go left and right to cross the bridge (you are going to Charlestown). At the end of the bridge curve right; at the light go right and then straight left at the bottom to Old Ironsides.

Pirates, not British warships, drove George Washington to establish a navy for the new country. That's right--Old Ironsides didn't fight in the Revolution, because she wasn't launched until 1797. But she and her five sister ships were needed to defend American shipping from troublesome pirates and marauding French vessels, in the West Indies and the Mediterranean.

Following gallant showing in several great battles against the British in the War of 1812--the mighty British navy!--she came to be called Old Ironsides. Cannon balls bounced off her dense hull of Georgia liveoak and New England white oak. She seemed invincible, and indeed in all her long history at sea she was never defeated, never even boarded.

Time, though, seemed more the enemy. In 1830, 1897, 1905, and on into the 1920's and 1950's, she was threatened with decommission, rotting, scrapping, and worst of all, use as a bull's eye in target practice.

But time was also the savior of U. S. S. *Constitution*. For gradually she had become a precious symbol of the newly-emerging power of the nation, of the great traditions of the sea and the navy, of the myths of American tradition. Time after time, the people and the Congress came to her rescue. The older she got, the more precious she became.

When you tour her decks, you will learn that she is still a commissioned ship, the oldest afloat in any navy in the world. The sailor who narrates your visit has applied for this two-year tour of duty, interviewed and specially chosen for the assignment. She or he will tell you that 309 people have died while serving on her, and so "It's an honor guard, and it makes us feel proud to serve on her."

Her crew observe all naval traditions, many of them going back hundreds of years to navies older than the United States; their conduct would be instantly recognizable to a sailor of the King's Navy of, say, 1820. These traditions bind her crew together, keep them mindful and proud of their membership in an ancient fellowship, and guarantee that the U. S. S. *Constitution* will continue to serve her country not only as a symbol of history but as an active source of pride.

MEDITATION
Traditions we observe make us aware of those who came long before us, those in our present with whom we share traditions, and those we trust will come after us.

Old Ironsides 77

FOR YOU TO DO AT OLD IRONSIDES

If you take the tour of Old Ironsides, see if you can observe any naval traditions in action.   Ask your sailor-guide about this.

What traditions do you observe, at work, in your neighborhood, in your family?   List a few.

1.

2.

3.

When you participate in these traditions, how does it make you feel? Do you think traditions are a hindrance or a help?   There's nothing more irritating than having someone say, "Oh, we've always done it that way, so no need to try anything new"!   But on the other hand, there is a delicious security in being part of a group and knowing exactly what's going to come next: now we sing this song, now we eat that food, now we read this together.

Good things about tradition:

Not so good things:

What are some American traditions?

What might be the value of these to American citizens?

At Old Ironsides, from its entrance by the rows of big black bollards, go up the hill, cross at the light, jog slightly left and then right onto Chestnut Street and from there left onto Adams Street. On you go to beautiful Monument Square.

So this is probably what you know about Bunker Hill: the British and the Americans had a battle here.

That's true. But there is more here than meets the eye, more than a big granite obelisk and a small green park.

It's June of 1775. Just two months earlier the Colonials had shown what they could do at the bridge in Lexington. The British were eager to strengthen their occupation of Boston. They thought to gain control of the big hill that looked down on Boston Harbor, Bunker Hill, just across the water in Charlestown. On Friday, June 17, we'll send some troops over there in boats and take it, they thought. That was the plan.

But on Wednesday the 15th, the Colonials got wind of this plan, and it was decided they should get to the hill ahead of the British. On the evening of Thursday, June 16, Colonel William Prescott gathered about 1,200 Colonial soldiers on the Cambridge Common, told them to pack light, and be absolutely silent as they marched under cover of darkness to Bunker Hill (well, yes, it was really Breed's Hill but who's quibbling at this point).

Once at the Hill, the men worked furiously through the night, setting up stone and wood fences and a kind of tiny dirt fort with low walls of six to eight feet high, called a redoubt, at the summit of the hill.

Where you are doubtless standing now.

June 17th was a hot day. When the British arrived they were astounded to find the Hill fortified. Not only that, but the Colonials had set up walls down on the beach, too, and some walls running down the hill from the redoubt to a swamp near the beach.   Other troops, from New Hampshire and Connecticut, had joined them.

Elsewhere at the Monument you can learn the story of that hot day of battle. How the British tried three times to take the Hill, and twice were turned back by the exhausted Colonials. How the Colonials, armed only with sticks and stones at the final assault, finally had to retreat.

So for the advancing British, what was there that day that wasn't immediately apparent? Snipers in the buildings of Charlestown, waiting to pick them off. Holes, rocks, hidden fences in the tall tough plants on the steep hill, maybe even thistles with prickers, all waiting to trip them up.   A horde of determined Colonials, a couple of thousand of them, at the top of the hill in their blasted little fort, picking off British officers with some accuracy.

On that day, what lay hidden from view for the Colonials?   They believed there would be reinforcements; instead, it turned out that they alone were to defend the Hill. There were British cannon firing on them from Copp's Hill across the water.   They weren't going to have enough ammunition for the long day, and their food and water would run out. Leadership was fragmented, and not everybody fought bravely.

From our vantage point in time we can see that indeed there was more in that day's engagement than met the eye at first. The British won but they lost.   Out of 2,200 British troops and officers that day, 268 were killed outright and 828 were wounded.   On the other side the Colonial force of 2,500 to 4,000 lost 115 killed and 305 wounded.

The British general Gage wrote to his superiors in London: "They [the Colonials] are now spirited up by a rage and enthusiasm as great as ever people were possessed of, and you must proceed in earnest or give the business up...The loss we have sustained is greater than we can bear..."

This great battle was a turning point, perhaps invisible at the time but quite clearly seen now. If you were British, you had to rise now to the occasion. If you were Colonial, you had to fish or cut bait, choose your side, and show what you were made of.

MEDITATION
This plot of ground is hallowed by the blood of nearly four hundred who died here that hot June day. Their blood is now hidden from view but that blood is here even though it is not visible. The small granite building at the base of the monument was originally intended as a place of meditation on their deaths and the bravery of those who fought here. Perhaps you can spend a few moments there in quiet thought.

FOR YOU TO DO AT THE BUNKER HILL MONUMENT

Imagine you are a Colonial soldier defending this hill. The buildings around you are gone. You can see the hillside in front of you covered with tall grass, some paths crossing through it, and then the houses and stores of Charlestown at water's edge. From your vantage point on the hill, behind your dirt and rock wall, you can see the flash of British cannon firing into the town, and smell burning wood. Smoke drifts in your direction.

Write a few thoughts that might be going through your mind as you wait for the British to march up the hill.

What are your feelings as you wait?

Sometimes only a small event can change your mind, and sometimes it takes something big. It's not always obvious that an event is a mind-changer, either. Think about a time when you did not have much of an opinion about an issue or situation, and then something happened to change your mind.

What was the issue you didn't care much about?

What happened to make you take a position on this issue?

Bunker Hill Monument

IN CLOSING

All of the historic places you have visited here in Boston are interesting and have extraordinary histories. But many people just look at them, hear or read a bit of their complex stories, take a picture, and move on to the next one. BUT THERE IS ALWAYS MORE THERE THAN MEETS THE EYE, and that "MORE" is what this book has attempted to help you discover.

Of all the sites in this book which you have visited, which one seems to you to have had the most to offer as you looked beneath its surface?

And what did you find, under the surface?

Thank you for walking in Boston, for looking beyond the bricks and mortar, and for perhaps learning something about your own place in history. Remember that today is tomorrow's history! What will you contribute?

ORDERING INFORMATION

If you would like to order additional copies of **Boston's Historic Places--So What?**, please send a check for $ 8.00 per copy, plus the completed shipping form below, to:

Jewelweed Books
30 Winslow St.
Cambridge MA 02138

Ship To:

Name: _____

Address: _____

_____

_____

_____

Email: _____

Number of copies ordered: _____

Amount enclosed: _____

Thank you for your interest!   If you have comments, email them to: jewelweedbooks@verizon.net